HIKING

PATAGONIA

2024

Unlock and discover the mesmerizing place of wild beauty, mountains, enormous glaciers, beautiful lakes at the southernmost point of South America.

Larry Lawler

Hiking Patagonia

Copyright © 2024 by Larry Lawler

All rights reserved. No part of this publication may be reproduced, distributed, or transmitted in any form or by any means, including photocopying, recording, or other electronic or mechanical methods, without the prior written permission of the publisher, except in the case of brief quotations embodied in critical reviews and certain other noncommercial uses permitted by copyright law.

TABLE OF CONTENTS

I. INTRODUCTION
- A. Overview of Patagonia
- B. Importance of Hiking in Patagonia
- C. Guide Purpose and Scope

II. TRIP PLANNING
- A. Best Time to Visit
- B. Entry Requirements and Permits
- C. Packing Essentials
- D. Health and Safety Tips

III. PATAGONIAN TRAILS
- A. Torres del Paine Circuit
- B. El Chaltén – Fitz Roy Trek
- C. Tierra del Fuego National Park

IV. GEAR AND EQUIPMENT

V. ACCOMMODATIONS

VI. FOOD AND WATER

VII. CULTURAL AND ENVIRONMENTAL CONSIDERATIONS

VIII. TRANSPORTATION

IX. PATAGONIAN WEATHER

X. ADDITIONAL RESOURCES
- A. Maps and Navigation Apps
- B. Useful Websites and Forums
- C. Recommended Reading

XI. CONCLUSION
A. Final Tips and Reminders
B. Share Your Experience

Hiking Patagonia

General Map Of Patagonia

Hiking Patagonia

I. INTRODUCTION

Patagonia is a mesmerizing place that invites travelers with its wild beauty, and we would like to extend a warm welcome to you as you enter its spectacular universe. With the help of this book, you will be able to discover the beauties of Patagonia through the lens of hiking, which is an activity that not only allows you to explore the rocky landscapes of the area but also brings you closer to the region's spirit. Let us go on this adventure together, where each step reveals a new landscape and each route tells a story of the splendor that nature has to offer at every possible moment.

A. Overview of Patagonia

Patagonia is a wide and diversified area that encompasses both Argentina and Chile. It is located at the southernmost point of South America. Tall mountains, enormous glaciers, beautiful lakes, and vast steppes are just some of the features that may be found in this region of extremes. Imagine the juxtaposition of rocky mountain ranges with placid fjords, and you have only scratched the surface of the breathtaking splendor that Patagonia has to offer.

Patagonia is a visual symphony that makes a lasting impression on all those who visit this region. From the recognizable peaks of Torres del Paine to the spectacular glaciers of Perito Moreno, Patagonia is a place that leaves an indelible mark. Its diverse combination of habitats, ranging from temperate rainforests to dry plains, contributes to the region's attractiveness. Patagonia is a playground for nature aficionados, a canvas painted with the brilliant colors of adventure.

B. Importance of Hiking in Patagonia

Hiking isn't only a pastime in Patagonia; it's the language through which you converse with the environment. Patagonia's rocky terrains are best experienced on foot, enabling you to immerse yourself in its raw, untouched beauty. The routes zigzag through a kaleidoscope of landscapes, affording hikers a front-row view of nature's great display.

Whether you're a seasoned trekker or a casual walker, Patagonia's routes appeal to all types of travelers. Hiking here is not only about reaching a goal; it's about the trip itself - the crunch of gravel under your feet, the fresh mountain air, and the excitement of seeing nature's treasures emerge step by step.

C. Guide Purpose and Scope

The objective of this book is to be your companion, sharing insights, ideas, and suggestions to make your Patagonian hiking experience unforgettable. We'll go into the nitty-gritty of trip planning, explain the secrets of the most compelling routes, and equip you with the information required to traverse this untamed paradise.

From identifying the ideal time to come and packing basics to immersing yourself in the local culture and ensuring your safety, this guide covers it all. Whether you're a lone traveler seeking isolation or a group of friends pursuing adventure, our purpose is to provide you with the information to make the most of your Patagonian hiking journey.

As we delve further into the tour, each part will unroll layers of knowledge, illuminating the complexities of Patagonia's trails, offering practical guidance on gear and lodgings, and immersing you in the cultural and environmental ethos of this unique place. So, buckle your boots, adjust your bag, and let's go on a voyage that promises not only a trek but an incredible expedition into the heart of Patagonia.

II. TRIP PLANNING

Welcome to the heart of your Patagonian experience — the key part of trip preparation. Getting the most out of your adventure begins with proper planning. In this area, we'll walk you through the ideal time to visit, entrance requirements, packing basics, and health and safety precautions, guaranteeing a flawless and delightful trip.

A. Best Time to Visit

Patagonia's weather is as varied as its scenery, so picking the proper time to come is crucial. The main hiking season normally extends from late spring to early autumn, approximately from October to April. During these months, the weather is more favorable, with warmer temperatures and longer daylight hours.

If you wish to observe the renowned burst of spring wildflowers, try traveling around November. For those desiring the tranquility of calmer paths, late autumn (March-April) would be appropriate. Keep in mind that Patagonian weather may be unpredictable, so layering is your friend. Be prepared for rapid shifts, and you'll be rewarded with breathtaking landscapes in every season.

B. Entry Requirements and Permits

Before going on your Patagonian expedition, acquaint yourself with the admission criteria. Ensure your passport is valid for at least six months beyond your anticipated travel date. Visitors from most countries do not need a visa for short trips, but it's necessary to verify the current restrictions before you go.

Many of Patagonia's national parks and prominent routes need permits, particularly during high season. Securing these licenses in advance is vital since they help limit tourist numbers and conserve sensitive ecosystems. Check official park websites or check with your tour operator to discover the permission requirements for your preferred trails.

C. Packing Essentials

Packing for Patagonia demands a combination of pragmatism and adaptability. Here's a summary of key items:

Clothing:

    Waterproof and windproof jacket

    Insulating layers (fleece or down jacket)

    Quick-drying, moisture-wicking base layers

    Sturdy, waterproof hiking boots

    Waterproof pants or hiking trousers

    Hat, gloves, and a buff or scarf for wind protection

Gear:

    Backpack with rain cover

Sleeping bag appropriate for cold temperatures

Trekking poles for stability on rough terrain

Headlamp with additional batteries

Multi-tool or knife

Others:

High SPF sunscreen and lip balm

Insect repellent

First aid kit with basic drugs

Water bottle or hydration system

Portable charger for electrical gadgets

Remember, packing light is crucial. Prioritize the fundamentals, and don't forget to verify the unique criteria of your selected terrain.

D. Health and Safety Tips

Patagonia's wild settings need special attention to health and safety. Here are some crucial tips:

Altitude Awareness:

Some pathways reach high heights. Acclimatize gradually to prevent altitude sickness.

Water Safety:

Drink only treated or bottled water to avoid waterborne infections.

Wildlife Caution:

Respect animals from a distance; certain species may be unexpected.

Emergency Contacts:

Save emergency numbers and know the location of the closest medical services.

Weather Preparedness:

Stay educated about weather predictions, and be ready for unforeseen shifts.

Group Travel:

Consider taking a guided tour for enhanced safety and local insight.

By sticking to these trip preparation principles, you create the groundwork for a pleasurable and secure exploration of Patagonia's stunning landscapes. Now, let's lace up those boots and get ready for an incredible voyage!

III. PATAGONIAN TRAILS

Welcome to the core of Patagonia's adventure - the trails that crisscross across its captivating scenery. In this segment, we'll go into one of the most legendary treks: the Torres del Paine Circuit. Get ready for a virtual journey, from the day-by-day schedule to the challenging terrain and intriguing places of interest that make this path a must-visit for every nature fan.

A. Torres del Paine Circuit

1. Day-by-Day Itinerary

Day 1: Starting the Journey

Begin your experience at the trailhead, where the air is packed with expectancy.

Hike through deep woodlands, enjoying the

sights of local fauna.

Reach the first campground, settling down with a view of the towering mountain peaks.

Day 2: Ascending to the Base of the Towers

Challenge yourself with a difficult trek to the foot of the renowned Torres del Paine.

Marvel at the dawn painting the granite towers with shades of pink and gold.

Descend to the next campground surrounded by spectacular sights.

Day 3: Navigating the Ascencio Valley

Traverse the Ascencio Valley, bordered by towering hills and glaciers.

Witness the raw beauty of the environment, as the wind whispers stories of old ages.

Camp under the great Patagonian sky, filled with stars.

Day 4: Into the Heart of the Circuit

Venture into the center of the circuit, encountering varied terrains.

Encounter tranquil lakes and wind-sculpted vistas that defy vision.

Rest in a conveniently positioned campground, surrounded by nature's symphony.

Day 5: The John Gardner Pass Challenge

Embark on a hard climb to the John Gardner Pass.

Revel in the stunning vistas of Grey Glacier and the Southern Patagonian Ice Field.

Descend to the Grey Valley, where turquoise lakes contrast with the glacial surroundings.

Day 6: Along the Shores of Lake Grey

Hike around the beaches of Lake Grey, with beautiful glacier views.

Witness icebergs drifting in the lake's crystal-clear waters.

Conclude the day at a campground affording a front-row seat to the glacier's beauty.

Day 7: Completing the Circuit

Complete the round with a last stretch amid lovely woodlands.

Cross magnificent suspension bridges, marking the completion of your adventure.

Return to the trailhead with a heart full of memories and a profound connection to Patagonia.

2. Terrain and Difficulty

The Torres del Paine Circuit offers a broad mix of terrains, giving both difficulties and benefits to hikers.

Mountain Passes: Navigate difficult ascents and

descents, notably the challenging John Gardner Pass.

Glacial Valleys: Traverse valleys sculpted by ancient glaciers, with ever-changing scenery.

Forest Trails: Immerse yourself in lush beech woods, filled with the sounds of nature.

Lakeside Paths: Follow the coastlines of beautiful lakes, each step affording postcard-worthy scenery.

High Plateaus: Experience the grandeur of high plateaus, where the wind whispers tales of loneliness.

While the circuit requires a moderate to high level of fitness, its ever-changing environment makes every stride a revelation.

3. Points of Interest

As you explore the Torres del Paine Circuit, be prepared to be charmed by these areas of interest:

Base of the Towers: Witness the stunning

granite spires of Torres del Paine up close.

Grey Glacier: Marvel at the vast length of the Grey Glacier and its glittering ice forms.

Southern Patagonian Ice Field: Stand near the John Gardner Pass for a panoramic picture of this gigantic ice field.

Lake Grey: Admire the ethereal beauty of Lake Grey, studded with floating icebergs.

Valle del Francés: Traverse the French Valley, flanked by towering peaks and hanging glaciers.

Each place of interest has a narrative, imprinting itself into your consciousness as a tribute to the untamed appeal of Patagonia. The Torres del Paine Circuit is more than a hike; it's an immersing excursion into the heart of one of Earth's remaining unspoiled places. So, lace up your boots and get ready to create your chapter in the tale of this incredible road.

B. El Chaltén – Fitz Roy Trek

Embark on a spellbinding trek along the El Chaltén - Fitz Roy Trek, a path that whispers stories of Patagonian splendor and untamed environment. In this part, we'll cover the trail's highlights, camping alternatives that link you with nature, and the wonderful encounters with animals that add a touch of enchantment to your trekking trip.

1. Trail Highlights

Prepare to be mesmerized as we uncover the highlights of the El Chaltén - Fitz Roy Trek, a trail that snakes through some of Patagonia's most spectacular vistas.

Majestic Fitz Roy: The path unfolds with stunning views of Mount Fitz Roy, an iconic peak that pierces the sky with its granite spires. Each step leads you closer to this Patagonian classic, exhibiting its varied features under shifting lighting.

Laguna Capri: Pause at Laguna Capri, a mirror-like lake reflecting the majesty of Fitz Roy. This tranquil place gives a fantastic vantage point for capturing the spirit of the countryside in your mind and camera.

Poincenot Campsite: Nestled within beech woodlands, Poincenot Campsite offers a serene refuge. Set against the background of Fitz Roy, it's the ideal spot to relax, rejuvenate, and absorb the beauty of your surroundings.

Cerro Torre: As you continue your trip, get views of Cerro Torre, another stunning mountain that contributes to the drama of the Patagonian vista. The fluctuating weather provides an ever-shifting tapestry of clouds and light around this magnificent peak.

Laguna de los Tres: The last rise gets you to the crown treasure — Laguna de los Tres. This blue jewel gives an incomparable glimpse of Fitz Roy's reflection in its waters, a treat that crowns your hiking efforts.

2. Camping Options

Experience the allure of Patagonian camping along the El Chaltén - Fitz Roy Trek. Each campground is deliberately positioned, giving not only a place to relax but also a link to the surrounding wildlife.

El Chaltén campsite: Start your adventure from El Chaltén, where the campsite offers minimal amenities and the possibility to mix with other hikers. Fuel up here before entering into the core of the route.

Poincenot Campsite: Set under the shadows of Fitz Roy, Poincenot Campsite provides a quiet ambience. Surrounded by beech trees, it's a fantastic area to savor the sounds of nature and tell tales over the campfire.

De Agostini camping: Situated near Laguna Capri, De Agostini is a lovely camping site with amazing views. Wake up to the dawn throwing its first light on Fitz Roy, making a stunning start to your day.

Camping Laguna Capri: For a more private experience, choose Camping Laguna Capri. It's a smaller location with a friendly environment, excellent for people seeking a calmer refuge among nature.

Wild Camping near Laguna de los Tres: For the brave spirits, consider wild camping near Laguna de los Tres for a night beneath the stars.

Remember to observe Leave No Trace principles to maintain beautiful nature.

3. Wildlife Encounters

The El Chaltén – Fitz Roy Trek brings you to Patagonia's abundant wildlife, bringing an element of surprise and magic to your trekking trip.

Andean Condors: Keep your eyes on the sky for the spectacular Andean condors flying above. With their enormous wingspan, these birds of prey negotiate the thermals, producing a stunning aerial dance.

Guanacos: Encounter guanacos, the wild relatives of llamas, grazing on the Patagonian steppe. Their beautiful presence against the background of the mountains adds to the genuineness of the walk.

Foxes: Patagonian foxes may make a strange

appearance along the path. These quick animals, with their bushy tails and acute eyes, are a joy to study from a respectful distance.

Birds: The area is filled with birds. Look out for the secretive Austral Parakeets, Magellanic Woodpeckers, and the lovely Torrent Ducks around water bodies.

Hares and rats: Patagonian hares and rats are commonly found in the grassy regions. Their presence gives a bit of wildness to the environment, as they go about their lives in peace with nature.

As you cross the El Chaltén – Fitz Roy Trek, these animal encounters become treasured memories, reminding you of the untamed grandeur that distinguishes Patagonia. Embrace the unexpected, listen to the whispers of the wind, and allow the animal tales to emerge as you go over this interesting route. The El Chaltén – Fitz Roy Trek is not simply a trip; it's a meeting with nature's beauties, where each step gets you closer to the heart of Patagonia's untamed soul. So, lace up your boots, and let the journey begin!

C. Tierra del Fuego National Park

Welcome to Tierra del Fuego National Park, a zone where the end of the globe meets stunning scenery. In this part, we'll cruise the picturesque roads that uncover the park's grandeur, discover the unique flora and wildlife that call this area home, and direct you to campsites and lodgings that enable you to immerse yourself in the spirit of Tierra del Fuego.

1. Scenic Routes

Tierra del Fuego National Park is a canvas painted with varied ecosystems, and its picturesque paths reflect the finest of this unspoiled nature.

Coastal Pathway: Begin your adventure via the Coastal Pathway, along the shores of the Beagle Channel. Marvel at the rough grandeur of the southernmost coastline, where the waves meet the rocks, and seagulls dance in the salty wind.

Pampa Alta Trail: Venture into the heart of the park on the Pampa Alta Trail, where wide vistas display the enormous splendor of the Fuegian steppe. Keep a look out for guanacos, the famous Patagonian creatures, as they graze in the wide areas.

Lapataia Bay: Reach the beautiful Lapataia Bay, where the mountains surround the peaceful seas. This is the southernmost point of the Pan-American Highway, affording a symbolic link to the great expanse of the Americas.

Valle de Lobos: Traverse Valle de Lobos, a valley called for the local sea lions that inhabit the neighboring islands. Watch these beautiful marine creatures as they sunbathe in the sun, creating a colorful show against the background of the channel.

Laguna Negra: Hike to Laguna Negra, a hidden beauty situated among ancient trees. The mirrored waters mirror the neighboring peaks, providing a serene haven that seems worlds away from the everyday rush.

2. Unique Flora and Fauna

Tierra del Fuego National Park is a refuge for biodiversity, presenting a tapestry of unusual flora and wildlife suited to the severe southern climate.

Magellanic woodlands: Walk through Magellanic woodlands characterized by lenga and trees. These resilient species tolerate difficult weather conditions, providing a home for various fauna.

Birdlife: Tierra del Fuego is a birdwatcher's heaven. Spot the bright Austral Parakeets, the magnificent Magellanic Woodpeckers, and the elusive Torrent Ducks along freshwater streams.

Mammals: Encounter the local beavers, brought to the region in the 20th century. Despite their questionable influence on the ecology, their dams produce unique wetland ecosystems.

Fuegian Red Fox: Keep a lookout for the Fuegian red fox, a local species with rust-coloured fur. These nimble animals may make a covert appearance as they explore the underbrush.

Marine Life: Explore the coastal regions to get

sightings of seals, sea lions, and seabirds. The Beagle Channel has a rich marine ecology that gives a maritime character to the park.

3. Campsites and Accommodations

Immerse yourself in the calm of Tierra del Fuego by picking the perfect campsites and lodgings that balance comfort with nature's embrace.

Camping Pipo: Situated near the park entrance, Camping Pipo provides minimal amenities and a handy position for visitors anxious to start their tour.

Lago Roca campsite: Set near the magnificent Lago Roca, this campsite offers a lovely location with services such as hot showers and a restaurant. Enjoy the sunset across the lake before retiring to your tent.

Hut and Lodge Options: For those wanting a

little more comfort, there are huts and lodges inside the park. These lodgings offer a pleasant getaway after a day of adventure, enabling you to relax in the middle of nature.

Ushuaia lodgings: If you prefer a base in Ushuaia, the adjacent city provides a selection of lodgings. From boutique hotels to quiet guesthouses, Ushuaia has alternatives for every tourist.

Tierra del Fuego National Park isn't simply a destination; it's a tribute to the rough beauty and tenacity of nature at the southern point of the earth. Whether you want to meander along the Coastal Pathway, marvel at the distinctive flora and wildlife, or relax beneath the starlit sky at a campground, each moment in Tierra del Fuego is a step into the untamed heart of Patagonia. So, with anticipation in your heart and the wind at your back, let's explore the wonderful landscapes of Tierra del Fuego.

IV. GEAR AND EQUIPMENT

Welcome to the practical aspect of your Patagonian journey! In this part, we'll dig into the crucial gear and equipment that will guarantee you're well-prepared for the unexpected beauty of Patagonia. From hiking requirements to wardrobe advice, camping gear, and camera equipment, let's gear up for an exciting vacation.

A. Essential Hiking Gear
Backpack:
Choose a comfortable and sturdy backpack with adequate storage for your requirements. Look for features like adjustable straps and cushioned hip belts for a tight fit.

Footwear:
Invest in robust, waterproof hiking footwear with strong ankle support. Ensure they are thoroughly broken in before your vacation to avoid blisters.

Navigation Tools:

Carry a thorough map and a dependable compass. For tech-savvy hikers, GPS equipment or smartphone applications with offline maps might be beneficial.

Waterproof Jacket:

Patagonian weather may be variable. Pack a waterproof and windproof jacket to remain dry and comfortable.

Layered Clothing:

Opt for moisture-wicking base layers, insulating mid-layers (fleece or down), and a breathable upper layer. Layering helps control body temperature under changing settings.

Headlamp:

A hands-free light with additional batteries is vital for early-morning or late-night trips and camping.

Trekking Poles:

Lightweight and adjustable trekking poles give

stability over uneven terrain and prevent pressure on your joints.

Water and Filtration System:
Carry a reusable water bottle and a water filter device or purification pills to guarantee a safe water source on the path.

First Aid Kit:
Pack a small first aid bag with basic things such as bandages, antiseptic wipes, pain relievers, and any personal prescriptions.

Multi-Tool or Knife:
A multifunctional multi-tool or knife may be beneficial for different activities, from cutting rope to making meals.

B. Recommended Clothing

Quick-Drying Clothing:

Choose moisture-wicking and quick-drying materials to be comfortable during strenuous activity.

Hiking Pants:

Lightweight and sturdy hiking pants are excellent, especially convertible for flexibility to changing conditions.

Warm Hat and Gloves:

Even in calmer seasons, temperatures may plummet. Pack a thick hat and gloves for cold mornings and nights.

Socks:

Opt for moisture-wicking and blister-resistant socks. Bring additional socks to keep your feet dry and comfy.

Sun Protection:

Pack sunglasses with UV protection, a wide-brimmed hat, and high SPF sunscreen to shelter yourself from Patagonia's fierce sun.

Buff or Scarf:

A multipurpose buff or scarf can shield your neck and face from wind and cold.

C. Camping Equipment

Tent:

Choose a lightweight and weather-resistant tent ideal for Patagonia's climate. Ensure it's simple to put up and sturdy.

Sleeping Bag:

Select a sleeping bag adequate for the forecasted temperatures. Consider a sleeping bag liner for increased warmth.

Sleeping Pad:

A comfy sleeping pad offers insulation from the chilly ground and increases your entire camping experience.

Cooking Equipment:

A tiny stove, cookware, and lightweight utensils are important for making meals on the road.

Food Storage:

Patagonia's fauna may be intriguing. Use a bear-resistant food canister or hang food in specific spots to deter unwanted visits.

Camping Stove and Fuel:

Choose a trustworthy camping stove that meets your requirements. Ensure you have adequate gasoline for the length of your journey.

Backpacking Pillow:

While it may seem like a luxury, a compact, inflatable traveling cushion may greatly enhance your sleep quality.

D. Photography Gear

Camera:

Bring a camera that matches your tastes and talents. Whether it's a DSLR, mirrorless, or a high-quality smartphone, documenting the moments is crucial.

Extra Batteries and Chargers:

Patagonia's magnificent vistas will have you reaching for your camera regularly. Carry additional batteries and chargers to keep your gadgets fueled.

Lens Options:

If you're using a DSLR or mirrorless camera, consider taking a flexible lens for landscapes and a zoom lens for animals or detailed images.

Tripod:

A durable and lightweight tripod is crucial for obtaining long-exposure images or supporting your camera in low-light circumstances.

Camera Rain Cover:

Given the uncertain weather, a rain cover will protect your camera from unexpected rain showers.

Lens Cleaning Kit:

Patagonia's atmosphere might be dusty or hazy. A lens cleaning kit guarantees your images remain sharp and clear.

Camera Bag:

Invest in a comfortable and weather-resistant camera bag to preserve your gear during treks and travel.

Now that you're armed with the fundamentals, your tour across Patagonia is primed for success. From the correct hiking clothing to comfy camping equipment and tools to capture the enchantment on camera, you're ready to enjoy nature. So, pack intelligently, explore wisely, and let the beauty of Patagonia unfold before your eyes.

V. ACCOMMODATIONS

Welcome to the world of Patagonian lodgings, where the possibilities vary from sleeping beneath the stars to charming lodges hidden amid nature. In this area, we'll investigate camping choices , mountain huts, lodges, and hostels, giving us something for every sort of explorer. Additionally, we'll give some helpful booking suggestions to ensure your stay matches perfectly with your Patagonian trip.

A. Camping Options

Wild Camping:

For the daring spirits, wild camping enables you to immerse yourself totally in the untamed environment of Patagonia. Be careful you observe Leave No Trace principles, preserve the environment, and secure relevant licenses.

National Park Campgrounds:

Many national parks in Patagonia have designated camping with modest amenities. These places provide a balance between wilderness immersion and convenience, making them suited for a spectrum of tourists.

Private Campgrounds:

Along famous hiking routes, you'll discover private campsites that may provide extra facilities such as hot showers, common areas, and the ability to meet other hikers.

Backcountry Camping:

Some paths, like those in Torres del Paine, give wilderness camping alternatives. These areas are more isolated, giving a unique experience for individuals seeking isolation and a closer connection with nature.

B. Refugios and Mountain Huts

Refugios:

are mountain shelters or cabins strategically positioned along famous walking routes. They give a more pleasant alternative to camping, giving bunk-style rooms, hot meals, and social areas.

Amenities at Refugios:

Refugios generally offer food, minimal sleeping accommodations, and common restroom facilities. Some may include extra facilities like hot showers, social rooms, and spectacular views of the surrounding surroundings.

Booking Refugios:

Due to their popularity, particularly during high seasons, it's advised to reserve in advance. This assures you have a guaranteed site and enables for better planning of your excursion.

Refugios in Popular Parks:

In well-trodden regions like Torres del Paine, play a significant role in hosting hikers. They provide a balance between the comforts of a bed and the raw appeal of the woods.

C. Lodges and Hostels

Lodges:

Lodges in Patagonia vary from small cabins to magnificent resorts. Nestled in gorgeous locales, they offer a pleasant and engaging stay for guests seeking a touch of luxury among nature.

Hostels:

Hostels provide budget-friendly rooms with communal amenities. They are common in gateway towns and cities, giving a social environment and an opportunity to engage with other tourists.

Amenities at Lodges and Hostels:

Lodges frequently come equipped with private rooms, eating choices, and activities. Hostels, on the other hand, may offer dormitory-style or private rooms and public facilities for socializing.

Gateway Town Accommodations:

When touring the region's communities like El Calafate or Ushuaia, resorts and hostels give a pleasant base for day treks into the surrounding natural treasures.

D. Booking Tips

Plan and Book in Advance:

Patagonia is a popular vacation, particularly during high seasons. Planning and arranging lodgings early in advance guarantees you acquire your chosen selections.

Flexibility in Itinerary:

While preparation is vital, including some flexibility in your schedule helps you to adjust to changing weather conditions or unforeseen possibilities along the road.

Consider Package Deals:

Some tour providers offer package offers that include lodgings, food, and guided activities. These may be handy and may bring cost savings.

Research Reviews:

Before making bookings, check reviews from other travelers. Their experiences may give useful insights into the quality of lodgings and services.

Pack Accordingly:

Depending on your selected lodgings, pack appropriately. Camping may need a tent and sleeping bag, whereas lodges and hostels may supply bedding.

Check Cancellation Policies:
Before confirming reservations, read the cancellation conditions. Life on the path may be unexpected, and having flexibility in your bookings is a vital benefit.

Local Recommendations:
Seek recommendations from locals or other tourists for hidden treasures and lesser-known hotels. Sometimes, the finest experiences come from staying in areas that aren't as extensively publicized.

In the wide area of Patagonian hotels, there's a housing choice for every sort of tourist. Whether you're inclined to the simplicity of camping, the community spirit of , the comfort of lodges, or the budget-friendly feel of hostels, each option adds a distinct element to your Patagonian experience. So, let's locate the right area for you to lay your head and dream beneath the southern sky.

VI. FOOD AND WATER

Welcome to the heart and soul of every expedition – nourishment. In this part, we'll explore the world of trail snacks, substantial meals on the move, keeping hydrated with water sources, and relishing in the tastes of traditional Patagonian food. So, take a food, hydrate, and let's begin on a tour through the flavors of Patagonia.

A. Trail Snacks and Meals
Trail Snacks:
Pack foods that give rapid energy and are simple to carry. Nuts, dried fruits, energy bars, and trail mix are wonderful alternatives. They're lightweight,

non-perishable, and can be enjoyed on the fly.

Dehydrated Meals:
Dehydrated meals are a backpacker's best buddy. They are lightweight, small, and need minimum preparation. Just add hot water, and you have a delicious dinner. Varieties vary from pasta meals to soups and stews.

Instant Oatmeal:
For a quick and hearty breakfast, try instant oatmeal. Add hot water, and in minutes, you have a pleasant and nutritious start to your day on the trail.

Nut Butter Packets:
Nut butter packages, like peanut or almond butter, are handy sources of protein and healthful fats. They are portable and may be spread over crackers or toast for a delicious snack.

Hard Cheese and Crackers:

Hard cheeses, such as cheddar or gouda, coupled with crackers, make a flavorful and energy-packed snack. Cheese is a wonderful source of protein and offers diversity to your trail diet.

Fresh Fruits:

While fresh fruits may have a limited shelf life, they may be a pleasant treat on the road. Apples, oranges, and berries may deliver a surge of vitamins and water.

Energy Gels and Chews:

For a rapid energy boost during the hard stages of the climb, try energy gels or chews. They are meant to give a quick supply of carbs.

Chocolate and Candy:

Indulge your sweet craving with chocolate or

sweets. They give a rapid supply of energy and maybe a morale booster during hard periods on the road.

B. Water Sources and Purification
Water Sources on the Trail:
Patagonia is endowed with magnificent water sources, including rivers, streams, and lakes. Plan your route to visit these natural water sites for replenishing your bottles.

Carry Sufficient Water:
While natural supplies are numerous, it's vital to transport adequate water between places. Consider the duration of your journey, the terrain, and weather conditions while calculating your water supply.

Water Purification Methods:
Even at supposedly pure water sources, it's smart to

cleanse your water. Options include water filters, purifying pills, or UV sterilizers. This precaution guarantees you remain protected from waterborne infections.

Hydration System:
Consider employing a hydration kit with a reservoir and a drinking tube. This enables you to drink water comfortably while on the go, promoting consistent hydration throughout the day.

Monitor Your Hydration:
Pay heed to your body's cues for hydration. Thirst, dark urine, and weariness might suggest dehydration. Stay ahead by drinking water continuously.

Hot Water Bottles:
In colder weather, having a thermos with hot water may be a comfortable addition. It offers warmth and may be used for warming beverages or

rehydrating dried foods.

C. Local Cuisine Recommendations

Asado (Barbecue):

Argentina's legendary barbecue, or , is a must-try. Indulge in luscious grilled meats, frequently paired with chimichurri sauce. The tastes are deep, and the community setting adds to the experience.

Empanadas:

These savory pastries are filled with a variety of ingredients, such as meat, cheese, or vegetables. Empanadas make for a simple and enjoyable snack on the run.

Locro:

A hearty stew, , is a classic meal commonly relished in colder times. It often contains corn, potatoes, beef, and other vegetables, producing a cozy and satisfying dinner.

Cordero al Palo (Spit-Roasted Lamb):

Patagonia is famed for its lamb dishes, and Cordero

al Palo is a highlight. The lamb is carefully cooked on a spit, resulting in soft and tasty flesh.

King Crab:

Along the coastal regions, notably in Ushuaia, delight in king crab, known locally as centolla. This dish shows the region's plentiful seafood.

Calafate Berry Treats:

Patagonia's distinctive calafate fruit is widely used in desserts. Try calafate jam, ice cream, or a typical calafate sour cocktail for a sample of the native tastes.

Mate Tea:

Embrace the Argentine tradition of mate tea. This traditional herbal drink is produced by steeping yerba mate leaves in hot water and drunk via a metal straw. It's a social activity and a means to engage with locals.

Dulce de Leche Treats:

Indulge in the delicious joy of dulce de leche, a caramel-like spread. Enjoy it on toast, pastries, or even as a filling in different desserts.

Patagonia not only satisfies your senses with spectacular views but also with a gastronomic adventure that reflects the region's numerous influences. From trail nibbles that keep you fuelled on the move to relishing local specialities, every mouthful adds to the depth of your Patagonian trip. So, whether you're snacking on a trail mix with a mountain vista or drinking mate with newfound acquaintances, let the tastes of Patagonia improve your adventure.

VII. CULTURAL AND ENVIRONMENTAL CONSIDERATIONS

Embarking on a Patagonian journey goes beyond the landscapes and trails—it entails respecting the rich culture and vulnerable nature of this pristine area. In this part, we'll dig into the significance of Leave No Trace principles, give ideas on connecting with local people, and throw light on animal conservation activities that help the preservation of Patagonia's unique ecology.

A. Leave No Trace Principles
Plan and Prepare:
Before heading out on your excursion, educate

yourself about the terrain, weather conditions, and rules. Adequate preparation promotes a smoother experience while reducing your influence on the environment.

Travel and Camp on Durable Surfaces:
Stick to designated routes and campsites to minimize undue harm to vulnerable ecosystems. Patagonia's plants and animals flourish when humans step softly on sturdy surfaces.

Dispose of Waste Properly:
Pack out everything garbage, including trash, leftover food, and litter. Leave no trace of your visit to conserve the unspoiled beauty of Patagonia for future generations.

Leave What You Find:
Refrain from plucking flora, upsetting animals, or removing rocks or relics. Preserve the natural and cultural legacy by leaving everything as you found it.

Minimize Campfire Impact:

While campfires may feel comfortable, their effect on the environment may be serious. Follow park restrictions about fires, and use a camp stove for cooking instead.

Respect Wildlife:

Observe animals from a safe distance and avoid feeding them. Human food may be damaging to animals, and keeping a respectful distance helps them preserve their natural habits.

Be Considerate of Other Visitors:

Keep noise levels moderate, surrender the route to others, and camp at a distance from other groups to ensure everyone can enjoy the calm of Patagonia.

Educate Yourself and Others:

Stay informed about local rules and environmental issues. Share your expertise with other tourists, establishing a community devoted to conserving the beauty of Patagonia.

B. Interacting with Local Communities

Respect Local Customs and Traditions:

Patagonia is home to different communities, each with its unique customs and traditions. Respect local traditions, whether in language, clothing, or social interactions.

Learn Basic Local Phrases:

While many residents in Patagonia understand Spanish, learning a few basic words may go a long way in building pleasant encounters and demonstrating respect for the local culture.

Support Local Businesses:

Contribute to the local economy by supporting small companies, purchasing locally created items, and eating at family-owned restaurants. Your decisions may have a beneficial influence on the communities you visit.

Seek Permission for Photography:

Before taking images of residents, particularly in

more isolated regions, obtain their permission. Some may prefer not to be photographed, and it's crucial to respect their desires.

Participate in Cultural Experiences:

If possibilities occur, partake in cultural events given by local communities. Whether it's a traditional dance, a craft session, or a local festival, these encounters give complexity to your experience.

Practice Responsible Tourism:

Be cognizant of the influence your presence may have on local communities. Practice ethical tourism by limiting interruptions, respecting private property, and being conscious of your cultural imprint.

Leave Feedback Responsibly:

If you have comments regarding your experiences, share them constructively. Positive feedback promotes and supports local companies, while constructive criticism may help improve services.

C. Wildlife Conservation Efforts

Follow Wildlife Guidelines:

Patagonia is a sanctuary for various fauna. Follow recommendations established by park officials on wildlife watching to safeguard both your safety and the well-being of the animals.

Avoid Feeding Wildlife:

Feeding animals may disturb their normal habits, impair their health, and promote reliance on human food. Resist the urge to feed animals, no matter how adorable or interested they may seem.

Support Conservation Organizations:

Many conservation groups work ceaselessly to maintain Patagonia's distinctive ecosystems. Consider supporting these programmes via contributions or volunteering to assist in the region's long-term conservation.

Participate in Citizen Science Programs:

Some parks and organizations operate citizen science activities. Participating in these activities may assist acquire useful data on animals and aid conservation efforts.

Stay Informed About Local Conservation Issues:

Stay informed on local conservation problems, such as habitat loss or risks to endangered species. Knowledge helps you to make decisions that accord with conservation aims.

Choose Responsible Tour Operators:

When picking tour operators, seek one's dedicated to ethical and sustainable operations. Operators who emphasize animal protection benefit the long-term health of the area.

Respect Wildlife Corridors:

Be mindful of animal corridors and migratory routes. Avoid interrupting these channels to enable animals to migrate freely and sustain healthy populations.

In the fragile balance between people and nature, your actions play a key part in conserving the cultural and natural diversity of Patagonia. By following Leave No Trace principles, respecting local people, and supporting wildlife conservation initiatives, you become a custodian of this beautiful place. So, while you cross the trails and connect with the people, let your adventure make a good and lasting influence on the fabric of Patagonia's cultural and natural legacy.

VIII. TRANSPORTATION

Embarking on a Patagonian expedition means navigating through the vast and stunning landscapes, and getting there is a voyage in itself. In this part, we'll discuss the ins and outs of transportation, from reaching Patagonia to local alternatives after you've been there, and the ease of shuttle services and transfers that make visiting this isolated area accessible and pleasurable.

A. Getting to Patagonia
Flights to Patagonia:

The voyage starts in the skies. Depending on your precise location in Patagonia, you'll likely fly into major airports such as El Calafate International Airport (FTE) Comandante Armando Tola International Airport (also in El Calafate), or Malvinas Argentinas International Airport (USH) in Ushuaia. These airports are well-connected to major cities in Argentina.

Gateway Cities:

Buenos Aires frequently serves as the principal entry to Patagonia. From Buenos Aires, you may take a domestic flight to provincial airports like El Calafate or Ushuaia. Some people can choose for a bus excursion from Buenos Aires to Patagonia towns, giving a picturesque option.

Domestic Flights:

Several airlines conduct domestic flights to Patagonian cities. Be careful to book your flights early, particularly during high seasons, to ensure the best schedules and costs.

Land Border Crossings:

If your itinerary involves both Chilean and Argentine Patagonia, consider crossing the land border. Popular crossings include the Paso de los

Libres in the north and the Cerro Castillo or Cardenal Samore crosses in the south.

Long-Distance Buses:

For those wanting a more intensive experience, long-distance buses are available from major towns to Patagonian hotspots. While the trip duration is longer, the stunning sights from the bus window give a distinct perspective of the area.

B. Local Transportation Options

Rental Cars:

Renting a vehicle allows the opportunity to explore Patagonia at your speed. Major vehicle rental firms operate in gateway cities and airports. Keep in mind that some isolated places may have gravel roads, so verify your vehicle is adequate for diverse terrains.

Local Buses:

Within Patagonia, local buses link cities, communities, and even national parks. While this alternative is affordable, schedules may be restricted, and preparing ahead is vital. Buses are a viable solution for shorter distances.

Shared Shuttles:

Shared shuttles travel between major attractions and are a pleasant choice for people who prefer not to drive. They offer door-to-door service, typically picking up and dropping off guests at hotels.

Taxis and Ride-Sharing Apps:

Taxis are accessible in metropolitan areas, and ride-sharing applications may also function in select cities. Confirm prices before commencing your travel, particularly for longer excursions.

Bicycle Rentals:

For the daring and eco-conscious, certain localities offer bicycle rentals. Exploring on two wheels lets you connect more directly with the environment.

C. Shuttle Services and Transfers

Airport Transfers:

Upon arriving at airports, particularly in El Calafate or Ushuaia, consider pre-arranging airport transportation. Many lodgings provide this service, allowing a flawless transfer from the airport to your starting point in Patagonia.

Inter-Park Shuttles:

In locations with many national parks, inter-park shuttles simplify the transition between sites. This is especially advantageous for touring the famed parks of Patagonia, such as Torres del Paine in Chile and Los Glaciares in Argentina.

Boat Transfers:

Given the region's abundance of lakes and rivers, boat transfers are a picturesque and effective form of transportation. These transfers typically link distant places, offering a unique view of Patagonia's natural splendor.

Transfers to Trailheads:

When going on multi-day walks, shuttle services enable transport to trailheads, reducing the need for extra transit arrangements. This ease enables you to concentrate on the trip ahead.

Customized Transfers:

Some tour companies offer personalized transfers, adapting the route to your unique schedule. Whether you're researching a certain itinerary or combining places, these services provide flexibility.

Guided Tours with Transfers:

Joining guided excursions frequently includes transportation, allowing a hassle-free way to discover Patagonia's attractions. Guides are informed about the area, giving insights that improve your visit.

Navigating the enormous expanse of Patagonia needs thorough consideration of transportation alternatives. From visiting the region via air or land to touring local places by buses, rental vehicles, or bicycles, the alternatives are wide. Shuttle services and transfers further increase the simplicity of travel, so you can concentrate on the awe-inspiring views that unfold before you. So, whether you're taking a flight to El Calafate or beginning on a magnificent bus tour across the Andes, let the travel to and within Patagonia become an intrinsic part of your wonderful vacation.

IX. PATAGONIAN WEATHER

Welcome to the ever-changing tapestry of Patagonian weather, where nature paints with an unexpected brush. In this part, we'll negotiate the seasonal climatic fluctuations that characterize this area and provide you with crucial weather readiness strategies. So, whether you're battling the blasts of the Andean wind or basking in the warmth of a Patagonian sun, let's decipher the factors that define your journey.

A. Seasonal Climate Variations
Spring (September to November):
As Patagonia releases from winter's hold, spring carpets the landscapes with colors of green and flowering wildflowers. Temperatures gently climb, ranging from pleasant to cold. Expect periodic rain showers, making waterproof clothing an important friend. This season uncovers a resurgence of life,

and hiking paths come alive with beautiful landscapes.

Summer (December to February):

Summer in Patagonia is a celebration of limitless sunshine, pleasant weather, and a boom of outdoor activities. Days are lengthy, with the sun sinking late in the evening. This is the ideal trekking season, given good weather for visiting classic treks like Torres del Paine Circuit and Fitz Roy. Be prepared for varied temperatures, from delightfully warm days to colder evenings.

Autumn (March to May):

As summer says goodbye, fall turns Patagonia into a painting of a golden leaf. The temperatures steadily decrease, providing a crisp and pleasant environment. Autumn is a calmer period, excellent for those seeking alone on the trails. Layers become needed when temperatures change, and a waterproof jacket is good for periodic rain.

Winter (June to August):

Winter lays a peaceful blanket over Patagonia, converting landscapes into a quiet winter paradise. While the weather might be frigid, this season displays a special appeal. Snow-covered peaks and frozen lakes offer a strange setting. Winter is wonderful for individuals who love the tranquil beauty of Patagonia, but it takes extra preparation for colder circumstances.

B. Weather Preparedness Tips

Layering is Key:

Patagonian weather is notable for its unpredictability. Layering helps you to adjust to changing situations effortlessly. Start with moisture-wicking base layers, add insulating layers for warmth, then top with a waterproof and windproof outer layer.

Waterproof Gear:

Invest in excellent waterproof clothing, including a jacket, jeans, and hiking boots. Patagonia's weather may be unpredictable, and being prepared for rain or unexpected showers assures a pleasant hike.

Wind Protection:

The fierce winds of Patagonia are part of its character. Pack wind-resistant clothes, such as a jacket, and consider wearing a buff or scarf to shield your face from windburn.

Sun Protection:

Even on gloomy days, the sun in Patagonia can be powerful. Pack sunglasses with UV protection, a wide-brimmed hat, and high SPF sunscreen to defend yourself from the sun's rays.

Hydration and Electrolytes:

Staying hydrated is vital in all seasons. Carry a reusable water bottle and refresh fluids frequently.

In warmer temperatures, try electrolyte pills to maintain a healthy balance.

Insect Repellent:

During warmer months, insects might be found in particular regions. Pack insect repellent to keep off mosquitoes and other biting insects, particularly in lowland locations.

Know Your Trail Conditions:

Stay updated about trail conditions and weather predictions for the exact regions you want to visit. Trail conditions might vary, and being prepared provides a safer and more pleasurable trip.

Emergency Kit:

Pack a modest emergency bag with necessities like a first aid kit, a multi-tool, a flashlight, and additional batteries. While the wide vistas are awe-inspiring, being prepared for unforeseen scenarios gives an added degree of protection.

Check Park Regulations:

Some parks in Patagonia have unique laws about hiking under certain weather conditions. Familiarize yourself with these standards to guarantee compliance and safety.

Local Advice:

Seek guidance from local guides, park rangers, or experienced hikers. Locals frequently provide significant insights into weather trends and may give practical recommendations for traversing the trails.

Stay Informed About Closures:

Occasionally, trail sections or parks may be closed due to weather conditions or maintenance. Check for updates before your travel to prevent surprise closures.

Patagonia's weather, like its scenery, is a dynamic force that influences your trip. By embracing the spirit of each season and preparing for the elements, you'll unleash the entire spectrum of

Patagonia's beauty. So, whether you're staring at a snow-covered mountain in winter or feeling the warmth of the summer sun on your cheeks, let the weather be a guiding aspect in your unique adventure into the heart of Patagonia.

X. ADDITIONAL RESOURCES

Welcome to the treasure mine of resources and information that will enrich your Patagonian experience. In this part, we'll dig into helpful tools, from maps and navigation applications that lead you through the wilderness to internet hubs where you can interact with other travelers. Additionally, we'll discuss suggested reading to go deeper into the rich tapestry of Patagonia. So, take your metaphorical compass, and let's provide you with the vital materials for an engaging adventure.

A. Maps and Navigation Apps

Physical Maps:

Start with a trustworthy physical map of the area. National Geographic and Patagonia Sur are noted for their comprehensive maps that include key hiking routes, national parks, and topographical features. These maps are essential for organizing your journey and having a better picture of the environment.

Digital Maps:

Embrace the ease of digital maps with applications like Gaia GPS, and Maps. me, or AllTrails. These applications enable offline access to precise maps, enabling you to navigate even in places with no internet availability. Download the maps for your preferred routes in advance and enjoy real-time tracking while on the go.

GPS Devices:

Consider carrying a specialized GPS gadget, such as those from Garmin or Suunto. These gadgets provide excellent tracking and maybe a solid backup to your smartphone. Ensure you're acquainted with the device's functionality and always carry spare batteries.

Compass:

While technology is amazing, a simple compass

remains a vital tool. It's lightweight, doesn't need batteries, and may be a lifesaver in case your electrical equipment fails. Familiarize yourself with fundamental navigation skills for greater confidence on the trail.

Trail Guidebooks:
Invest in trail guidebooks suited to the locations you wish to visit. Authors like Lonely Planet and Bruce Chatwin have authored extensive guides that give insights into the routes, sites of interest, and practical recommendations. These guidebooks function as companions on your trip.

B. Useful Websites and Forums

Wikiloc:
Wikiloc is a community-driven website where hikers exchange GPS footprints of their paths. Browse through the huge database to locate user-generated routes, reviews, and images. It's a

terrific resource for locating hidden treasures and lesser-known paths.

Patagonia Forums on Lonely Planet:

The Lonely Planet forums include special areas for Patagonia, where visitors exchange information, share experiences, and ask questions. Engaging with this group delivers real-time insights and direct guidance from other travelers.

REI Co-op Community:

The REI Co-op Community is an online center for outdoor lovers. Explore the forums to discover conversations on gear suggestions, trail conditions, and trip reports. It's a useful venue to engage with a bigger community interested in outdoor hobbies.

Patagonia Weather Websites:

Stay informed on weather conditions using websites like Windy and Weather.com. These tools include precise predictions, wind patterns, and satellite images, enabling you to plan your activities based on current and forecasted weather.

Trail Conditions Reports:

Websites like Sendero Chile give up-to-date trail conditions and information on numerous routes throughout Chile. Before starting on a journey, check these reports for the latest updates on trail accessibility, closures, or other possible problems.

Local Tourism Websites:

Visit the official tourist websites of Patagonian regions and national parks. These websites typically contain crucial information about park laws, access fees, and seasonal changes. Examples are CONAF (National Forest Corporation) in Chile and Administración de Parques Nacionales en Argentina.

C. Recommended Reading

"In Patagonia" by Bruce Chatwin:

Immerse yourself in the exquisite words of Bruce Chatwin as he narrates his trek across the landscapes of Patagonia. This classic travel tale delivers a combination of adventure, history, and cultural insights.

"The Old Patagonian Express" by Paul Theroux:

Join Paul Theroux on a spectacular train ride across South America, including the isolated areas of Patagonia. His sharp insights and writing ability make this travelog an intriguing read.

"The Revenant" by Michael Punke:

While not directly about Patagonia, this compelling tale is based on the experience of frontiersman Hugh Glass. The account of surviving in the harsh outdoors conveys a vivid feeling of the obstacles one can confront in untamed areas.

"The Whispering Land" by Gerald Durrell:

Durrell, famed for his animal excursions, takes readers on a hilarious and instructive tour across Patagonia. This book gives a distinct viewpoint on the region's vegetation and animals.

"The Tunnel" by Ernesto Sabato:

This Argentine classic goes into the psychological environment, probing the mentality of an artist. Set in Buenos Aires yet with connections to Patagonia, the story portrays the enigmatic and intriguing elements of the place.

"Patagonia: A Cultural History" by Chris Moss:

For anyone interested in the cultural fabric of Patagonia, Chris Moss's investigation of the region's history, mythology, and present-day realities delivers a detailed and interesting perspective.

Armed with these materials, your trip across Patagonia turns into a well-informed and enjoyable experience. From navigating the trails with digital accuracy to interacting with other travelers in online groups and digging into the cultural and environmental narratives via suggested reading, each resource adds a layer to the tapestry of your Patagonian experience. So, whether you're perusing a map beneath the Southern Cross or swapping trail experiences in a virtual forum, let these tools be your friends on the path less traveled.

XI. CONCLUSION

As your virtual tour guide across the vast and awe-inspiring landscapes of Patagonia, we've gone on a trip that encompassed towering peaks, pristine trails, and the colorful cultural fabric of this unique area. As we near the finish of our journey, consider this your chance to ponder, prepare, and relish the memories you'll bring from Patagonia. Let's end our voyage with some last suggestions, reminders, and a shared moment of experience.

A. Final Tips and Reminders

Flexibility is Key:

Patagonia is notorious for its ever-changing weather and unexpected situations. Embrace the spirit of flexibility in your ideas. Sometimes, unexpected diversions lead to the most unforgettable discoveries.

Respect Nature and Local Communities:

The beauty of Patagonia comes with a duty to conserve it. Adhere to Leave No Trace principles, respect local cultures, and encourage sustainable tourism practices. Your efforts help to the preservation of this precious habitat.

Check Park Regulations:

Each national park in Patagonia may have special restrictions. Before starting on a path, check the park's official website or visitor center for the latest information on admission fees, camping permits, and any limitations.

Stay Informed About Trail Conditions:

Trail conditions might vary depending on the season, recent weather, and park upkeep. Stay informed by visiting local websites, and forums, and, if possible, conversing with park rangers or experienced trekkers.

Pack Wisely:

Your packing list is your survival gear on the path. Double-check your gear, ensuring you have adequate layers for diverse conditions, and carry basics like a first aid kit, food, and a reusable water bottle.

Connect with Locals:

Patagonia is not simply a location; it's an experience molded by its people. Take the time to interact with people, whether it's a quick talk with a store owner or a shared mate with other hikers. These interactions offer dimension to your adventure.

Capture Moments, Not Just Photos:

While the scenery is surely stunning, try to put the camera down periodically and absorb yourself in the experience. The memories you make are as essential as the images you shoot.

Safety First:

Prioritize safety on the trails. Inform someone about your trip, have a map and compass, and be cautious of your physical limitations. If situations get hard, don't hesitate to turn back.

B. Share Your Experience

Create a Travel Journal:
Consider maintaining a trip notebook to capture your experiences, ideas, and feelings. Reflecting on your travel increases the personal connection you have with the locations you've visited.

Share Your Photos and Stories:
Share the beauty of Patagonia with friends, family, and other travel lovers. Whether via social media, a blog, or a casual chat, your photographs and tales encourage others to go on their journeys.

Stay Connected with the Community:
If you interact with online forums or social media groups, continue expressing your views and experiences. Your expertise provides a great resource for future tourists seeking help.

Encourage Sustainable Practices:

As an ambassador of Patagonia, support sustainable habits among your travel companions. Share the significance of responsible travel and having minimum damage to the environment.

Plan Your Return:

Patagonia has a magnetic draw that frequently compels tourists to return. As you wave goodbye, consider planning your future excursion. Whether it's returning familiar routes or discovering new places, Patagonia welcomes you back with open arms.

In the fabric of Patagonia, each tourist crafts a unique tale. As you complete your tour, bring the spirit of adventure, respect for the environment, and the warmth of shared experiences with you. Whether you're looking at the famous peaks of Fitz Roy, hiking the trails of Torres del Paine, or just musing on the expanse of the Southern Cone, let Patagonia's charm stay in your heart. Until our paths intersect again, may your experiences be as limitless as the places you've visited. Safe travels!

Made in the USA
Las Vegas, NV
17 December 2024